the Art of Creating

The ABC Basic Lessons

WHITE STAR PUBLISHERS

Contents

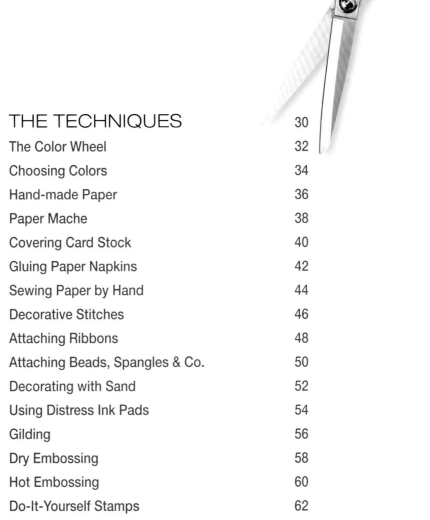

Introduction

Before starting with your own creative projects, learning how to decorate your home with light-hearted and original décor, rendering your holiday celebrations unique with sparkling decorations, embellishing a child's bedroom in a fun and colorful way, or making boxes, packets, invitations, cards, albums, notebooks and containers that are different and creative every time, you must learn the basic techniques involved and get well acquainted with the materials and tools that you will need. This volume allows you to do just that. A true creative reference guide, it provides you with detailed but at the same time easy to understand information about how to choose the right materials and the best way to utilize them, how to employ the tools of the trade and how to choose colors and select decorative elements. Learning these secrets will enable you to begin your creative projects and see your unique ideas slowly take shape.

The Materials

White Paper

White paper has multiple applications and can be used in many projects. To make the best use of this paper, learn to distinguish its different types and their characteristics!

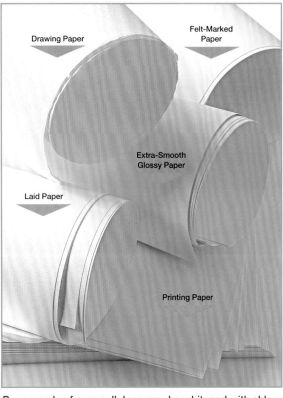

Paper Composition
The most common material used to make paper is cellulose pulp, which is obtained by from the fibrous portions of soft woods such as pine and poplar. Good quality paper has a variable percentages of cotton fibers, while the most prized paper is composed of 100% cotton.

Storing Paper
For creations that will not alter with time, give preference to paper that has a neutral pH and is free of chlorine (ECF Elemental Chlorine Free), acids (Acid Free) or lignin, the substance that keeps wood fibers together but tends to cause yellowing of paper with time if not eliminated during paper manufacturing. In addition, store sheets of paper in a dry location away from light.

Paper made of pure cellulose may be whitened with chlorine, which has a significant environmental impact, or with oxygen. In the latter case, the paper is labeled "ecologic."

Glossary

Watermark
It appears as an image composed of lines or areas lighter in color than the rest of the paper, visible when the held up against a light source. The watermark, which varies in definition with paper type, is created by differing the amount of pulp deposited in the desired areas.

Grammage
Grammage corresponds to the weight of a 1 m² piece of paper. For example, 1 m² (3.3 sq. ft.) regular printing paper has a weight of 80 g (2.8 oz.), while 1 m² of watercolor paper can weigh as much as 300 g (10.5 oz.). Blocks of paper include indications of the grammage on their packaging. Based on its grammage, paper is divided into paper, card stock and cardboard.

Texture
Texture refers to the appearance of the paper's surface, which is conditioned by the distribution, shape and dimensions of the surface roughness (for example coarse or fine, regular or irregular texture). The term "textured" is used above all when texture is used to create an artistic effect, for example "striped" or "hammered" paper.

Printing Paper

This paper is indispensable for printers and photocopiers. Choose paper with a grammage of 80 g/m2 for every day use, printing, and for photocopying shapes and diagrams. For coating objects, use paper with grammages of 90, 100 or 100 g/m2 because they are easier to glue.

Standard Paper Formats

ISO 216 standard defines the most common paper formats:

- A0 (841x1189 mm, 33.1x46.8 in.); drafting, posters
- A1 (594x841 mm, 23.4x33.1 in.); drafting, posters
- A2 (420x594 mm, 16.5x23.4 in.); drawing, diagrams, large charts
- A3 (297x420 mm, 11.7x16.5 in.); drawing, diagrams, large charts, newspapers
- A4 (210x297 mm, 8.3x11.7 in.); letters, magazines, catalogues, standard printing paper
- A5 (148x210 mm, 5.8x8.3 in.); notebooks

Felt-Marked Paper

This paper can be felt-marked on one or both sides. The marked surface has a light texture obtained using a marking felt. Paper that is marked on the front and smooth on the back has several uses. To avoid variations in color, don't confuse the sides of the paper while working on a project. The rough and smooth sides of the same piece of white paper will reflect light differently hence, the color may appear different.

Laid Paper

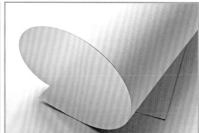

This paper is characterized by stripes and veins visible when held up to a light. The pattern of parallel lines is left by the laid wires attached to the frame of the paper making mold (parallel to the long side), which gather the cellulite fibers. The laid wires are linked to each other and to the ribs (wood rods attached to the frame of the mold parallel to the short side) by the chain wires. The pattern left by the wires is called the laid.

Drawing Paper

This paper it is particularly suitable to the various painting and drawing techniques (watercolor, tempera, charcoal, graphite, crayons, pastels, markers etc.). It can have a smooth or coarse surface.

Extra-smooth Glossy Paper

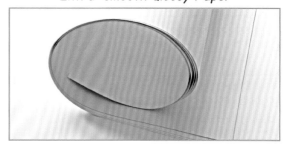

It can add a brilliant spot of white. It is very smooth on both sides. Handle it with care because it easily stains if it comes into contact with our skin, which has an acidic pH. To be able to erase pencil lines, use a B pencil and don't press down too hard.

9

Natural Paper

Natural paper is made by hand from a mixture of plant fibers that make it quite strong. It can be colored or patterned, with or without embedded material.

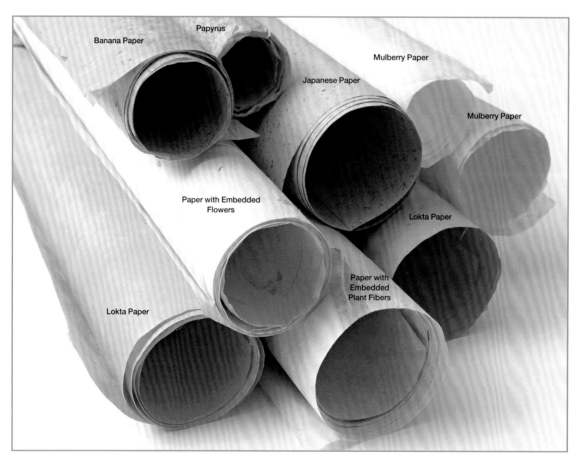

Banana Paper

Papyrus

Mulberry Paper

Japanese Paper

Mulberry Paper

Paper with Embedded Flowers

Lokta Paper

Paper with Embedded Plant Fibers

Lokta Paper

Standard Paper Formats

- ▶ A0   33.1x46.8 in.
- ▶ A1   23.4x33.1 in.
- ▶ A2   16.5x23.4 in.
- ▶ A3   11.7x16.5 in.
- ▶ A4   8.3x11.7 in.
- ▶ A5   5.8x8.3 in.
- ▶ A6   4.1x5.8 in.

Unlike machine made paper, which has smooth edges, handmade paper has four uncut edges.

Gluing Thin Paper
For natural paper with grammages below 50 g/m2, don't use Elmer's glue. Instead, use a glue stick, spray adhesive or double-sided adhesive tape.

Mulberry Paper

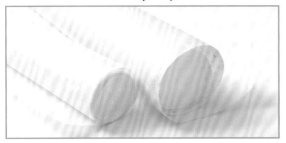

It is made from the bark of the paper mulberry tree. To maintain its "natural" appearance it is best to tear it instead of cutting with a utility knife: position a ruler on the paper, mark the paper with a wet paintbrush along the ruler and carefully tear the paper into two. Mulberry paper has a low grammage (25g/m2) and a characteristic texture with clearly visible fibers.

Lokta Paper

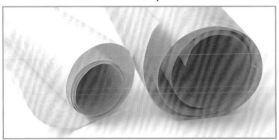

This type of paper – originally produced exclusively for Tibetan manuscripts – is made from the inner bark of a shrub that grows in the forests of Nepal, the Daphne papyracea, also called the Lokta bush. With grammages ranging from 30 to 130 g/m2, its irregular texture creates "plays" of transparencies highly sought for lampshades and greeting cards.

Japanese Paper

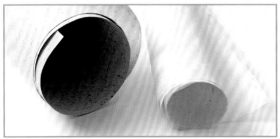

Japanese paper, called Washi, is produced from different shrubs such as mulberry, hemp and bamboo. It is particularly long lasting and resistant, and suitable for making greeting cards.

Writing on Plant-Based Paper
Most types of natural paper are quite absorbent because their surfaces have not been smoothed to render it suitable for writing and stamping. Therefore, before writing or stamping with pens, markers or inks, which may run and form blots just as they would on blotting paper, it is best to first perform a test on a small scrap piece of the chosen paper.

Papyrus

It is composed of thin strips taken from the stem of the papyrus plant. The strips are submerged in a water solution for a certain period and then laid out adjacent to each other. A second layer of strips oriented in the other direction is placed on top. The process is repeated until the correct thickness is achieved. Once dry, the strips bind to each other. In fact, this type of paper is very resistant, in addition to being very decorative. It can be used to cover albums or as a background for scrapbook pages.

Other Natural Papers

Other natural papers are made from flax, straw, rice or banana fibers. They may have natural materials such as seaweed, flowers, leaves and blades of grass embedded in them. These papers are made by hand therefore, before cutting or gluing, always perform a test to see how they will behave with the tools and materials you will be using.

Translucent Paper

Known in crafting as vellum paper, today, it is produced in many colors and even with embossed and stamped patterns. It is a glossy translucent paper heavier than tracing paper. Vellum paper can be used for a wide range of projects such as decorations and prized greeting cards.

Translucent paper is available in a variety of sizes and in the form of sheets, blocks, rolls or bags.

Suggestion Translucent paper stains easily when handled due to skin transpiration: for more delicate steps, insert another piece of paper between the translucent paper and your hands shifting it as needed while you work.

Translucent paper is delicate but long lasting at the same time! It is as resilient as regular paper of the same grammage but has some important differences: its fibers are fragile (once a fold is scored, the crease will remain very visible, with no possibility of correction; if handled too much the sheet may tear), and on contact with water, it stains, warps and swell irreparably.

Tracing

Tracing paper, with a low grammage (42g/m2), is cheap and perfect for tracing. Even sheets of 90 g/m2 are greatly recommended: due to their greater resistance, a design can be traced several times without risk of the paper tearing. For tracing, use a pencil with a medium hardness (2B, B or HB).

Gluing

Gluing translucent paper presents two problems, its sensitivity to humidity and its translucency: liquid adhesives cause it to warp, while double sided tape remains visible. To glue it "invisibly," completely transparent glue dots for vellum are particularly useful. Alternatively, position drops of glue or pieces of double-sided tape in locations that will later be covered by letters, photos or decorations. Spray adhesive gives variable results depending on the quality and composition of the paper therefore, do some tests before using it in your projects.

Cutting

Translucent paper can be cut with scissors or a utility knife. You can also punch shapes in it using craft punches but be careful: paper with lower grammage tends to tear before the blade can cut it. Always do some tests on scraps of paper before proceeding.

Grammage
Varies from 42 g/m2 (tracing paper) to 200g/m2. For tracing, use tracing paper or sheets with a grammage of 90 g/m2 when possible.

Folding

Never use a utility knife to score a fold: the paper will be irreparably cut! Instead, position a ruler on the fold to be scored, insert the bone folder under the paper and pass it along the ruler. Then fold, pressing down gently with your nails.

Tearing

For an irregular effect along one side, just tear the paper with your hands. For a "guided,", more linear tear, fold the paper as explained in the previous paragraph and gently pull apart applying uniform pressure.

Assembling

To secure translucent paper, instead of glue, you can use decorative elements such as small wood clothespins, paper fasteners, rivets, paper clips, embroidery thread etc.

Stamping

Inks do not dry quickly on translucent paper. Do a test on a scrap of paper, leaving it to dry while you complete your project. To make sure the ink will not smear, drag you finger over the stamped motif.

13

Paper Stock

Paper stock is a fundamental element for your creations: it allows to add rigidity to backgrounds, make frames, create depth and decorate in 3D. It exists in numerous types, each with its own properties: appearance, rigidity, durability, grammage etc.

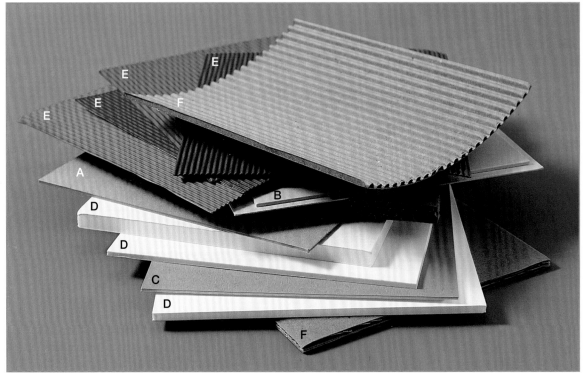

(A) Chipboard (B) Finnboard (C) Mat Board (D) Foam Board (E) Corrugated Paper (F) Corrugated Cardboard

Suggestion

Squaring and Cutting

Some types of cardboard have slightly rounded edges. Before starting a project requiring precise measurements, it is advisable to draw lines 1/4 in. (5 mm) from the edges with the help of a triangular ruler. To draw a line on corrugated paper, align one edge of the triangular ruler with the ribbing. Cut using a utility knife, making sure to replace the blade as soon as it starts to dull.

Grammage

The term "grammage" refers to the weight of a piece of paper with a surface area of one square meter. Based on grammage, paper stock is divided into paper, cardstock and cardboard. Cardstock, which is a kind of heavy paper, has a grammage between 150 and 450 g/m2 (thickness above 1/64 in., 0.3 mm). Cardboard (excluding foam board) has a grammage between 450 and 1200 g/m2.

Chipboard

Chipboard is made from recycled paper stock. It is very hard, cheap and recommended for all projects. Often, its pH is acidic. Its thickness varies 1/16 to 1/8 in. (1.5-3 mm). If you need to cover it with very thin paper, coat it with white acrylic or "gesso" until the color of the board is not visible through the paper or no longer alters its color.

Finnboard

Finnboard is a unique board, similar to plywood made from wood pulp. It is very hard and has a neutral pH. Its thickness varies from 1/32 to 1/8 in. (0.7-3.5 mm). It has the same uses as chipboard but costs more.

Mat Board

Mat board is often used in picture framing, but can also be used to make album pages and covers, as well as boxes. It is made by gluing two sheets of white or colored paper onto either side of a white board. If the facing sheets are colored, the white core is visible: keep this in mind and color it using an ink pad of the same color as the facing sheets.

Storage

To prevent deformation, store cardboard and cardstock completely flat. If you don't have enough space, position the sheets vertically but secure them together tightly in a portfolio (only foam board can be stored in a vertical position without risk).

Gesso

Gesso is a fluid white coating used in Italy for finishing smooth walls that can also be used to whiten many backing materials (cardboard, wood, canvas for painting). It is best to apply it with a wide, flat brush, in order to speed up the process.

Foam Board

Foam board, like mat board, is part of the laminated board family because it is composed of a polystyrene core coated on either side with paper. Its thickness varies from 1/16 to 3/8 in. (2-10 mm). It's easy to cut: a simple utility knife is sufficient. When cutting foam board, keep the blade perfectly perpendicular to the surface, or the cut will result beveled.

Corrugated Paper

It's available in many colors, in sheets or rolls. Sheets are easier to work with because when rolled, the paper retains the curve and becomes difficult to flatten. Folds perpendicular to the ribbing are more solid and sharp than those that are parallel.

Corrugated Cardboard

Normal corrugated cardboard is composed of a central corrugated layer sandwiched between two flat sheets. Double wall corrugated cardboard contains three flat sheets: two glued to the outside and one in the center, between two corrugated sheets. These cardboards can be purchased in sheets as well as taken from packaging boxes.

Transparent Plastics

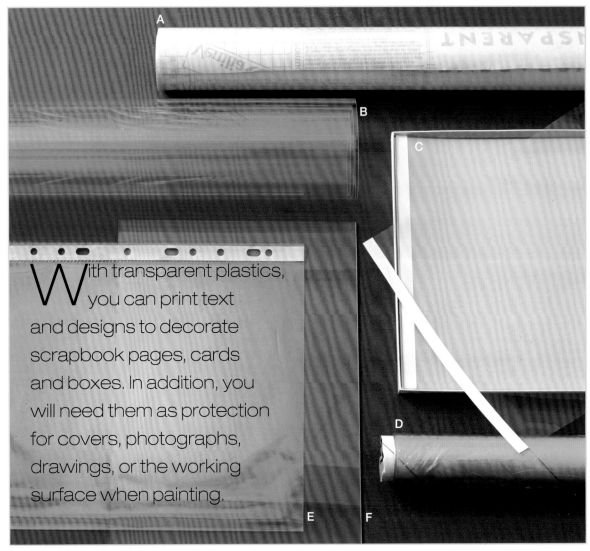

W ith transparent plastics, you can print text and designs to decorate scrapbook pages, cards and boxes. In addition, you will need them as protection for covers, photographs, drawings, or the working surface when painting.

A - Transparent adhesive film. B - Acetate.
C - Tracing film. D - Plastic wrap.
E - Polypropylene bag. F - Plexiglas sheet.

Suggestion

Coloring Plastics

You can color or draw designs on plastic using a permanent marker, opaque acrylic paint (including dimensional paint!), or transparent, glossy glass paint.

Printing

Compose the text on a computer and print onto transparency film (available both for inkjet and laser printers). Transparency film can be decorated with stamps using ink pads for impermeable surfaces.

Framing

Before framing, protect a photograph or a drawing with a rectangle of acetate, which can be cut with a utility knife or scissors, or Plexiglas. To cut the latter, score the cutting line repeatedly with a utility knife. Place the sheet on a working surface aligning the scored line with the edge and press down with force for a clean break.

Make a Shaker Box

Make transparent shaker boxes full of glitter, rhinestones, spangles, tiny shells, flowers and so on, for decorating a scrapbook page or a card. Cut two rectangles from the polypropylene bag or from an acetate sheet. Seal three sides with double-sided adhesive tape, fill the packet and seal the last side.

Gluing

To glue onto a backing, you can use quick-drying adhesive or adhesive tape. For gluing onto the front, use invisible glue dots or hide the glue with decorations. You can also attach plastic elements with rivets or paper fasteners.

Protecting

Protect the cover of an album or a notebook with transparent adhesive film. When working on a paper mache project, protect the base form with plastic wrap. Polypropylene bags and Plexiglas will serve to protect the working surface during your painting or modelling projects.

Suggestion

Don't throw away scraps of transparency and acetate sheets: you can use them to make labels, decorations or small windows.

Balsa Wood

This is a soft wood that is easy to cut and to paint. Available in sheets of various thicknesses and strips, you can use it to make backgrounds or frames. Rods of this wood cut into pieces can also be used to bind the pages of an album.

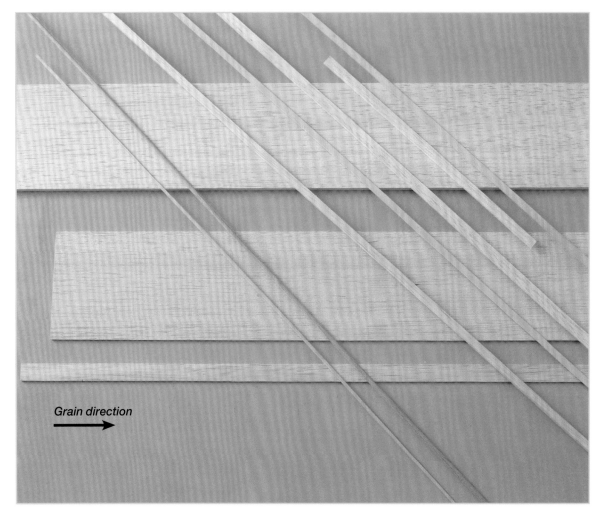

Grain direction

3 ft. (1 m) long rods, strips and sheets of balsa wood with thicknesses from 1/8 in. (3 mm) to several centimeters.

Balsa wood can be perforated with a riveting tool.

Painting

Balsa wood can be painted just like other types of wood. If you don't want to cover the veining, use an impregnating or highly diluted acrylic paint. For a full color lacquer effect, use undiluted acrylic paint. Spread the paint with a wide brush and allow to dry for several hours, because this wood absorbs a lot of liquid.

Cutting

Cut balsa wood with a utility knife equipped a new blade. Score the cut line repeatedly to ensure the wood fibers are cut cleanly. To cut hinge pins, use a miter box (available for sale in plastic and wood) and a back saw.

Gluing

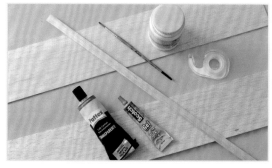

Balsa wood is best glued with fast-drying or neoprene-based adhesive. For very small objects, you can use double-sided tape. If you use Elmer's glue, the wood must be dried under a weight.

Making a Frame

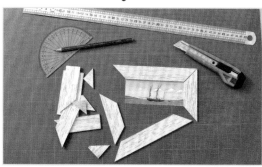

Take four strips of balsa wood and cut the ends at 45° angles. Glue each strip around the drawing or photograph to frame. Lightly sand the frame with extremely fine sand paper to make the surface uniform and smooth. If you want the wood to be colored, paint it before assembling the frame. To give "depth" to the frame, stack several strips of wood.

Suggestion

Mark the Grain Direction

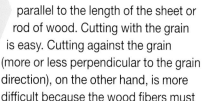

Grain direction

Balsa, like all types of wood, has a grain direction: the wood is cut in the direction of the grain, i.e. the wood fibers are parallel to the length of the sheet or rod of wood. Cutting with the grain is easy. Cutting against the grain (more or less perpendicular to the grain direction), on the other hand, is more difficult because the wood fibers must be truncated.

Making a Background

Cut a backing from chipboard or foam board. Paint strips of balsa wood with different shades of the same color. Allow to dry and cut the strips into rectangular or square pieces. Glue the pieces to the backing. Remove excess wood by cutting flush with the backing. Color the edges of the wood with an ink pad.

Modeling Clays

Modeling clay can be used to make beads, buttons and different embellishments for your projects. Different color clays can be mixed together to obtain beautiful effects. As a finish, you can coat the clay with a matte or glossy glaze.

Modeling clays can be cut and modeled to create a great variety of objects.

Objects Made with Cutters

Roll out the clay with a roller (to get a surface of consistent thickness, place the paste between two skewers). Take a cutter and press it hard into the clay to cut completely through. To make buttons, use a plastic bottle cap.

Perforated Objects

Make holes in buttons and beads with toothpicks. To ensure that the bead does not deform use two toothpicks: push one through the bead without having it exit the other end then pull it out; insert the other toothpick into the exit hole and push towards the other side.

Molded Objects

Take a small portion of clay and place it into the desired mold cavity. Pass the roller over it. Cut away any clay that spills over the edges of the mold. Extract the clay (if it does not come out easily, place the mold into the freezer for a few seconds).

Multi-Colored Objects

You can use modeling clay to create multi-colored objects. Shape rolls from different color clay (or use an extruder with a die). Overlap and twist them together. Roll out the resulting piece of clay with a roller and cut out the shapes.

Hand-Modelled Objects

To make beads, simply roll a small ball of clay with the palms of your hands. To make elongated beads, form a roll with your fingers on a working surface then cut into pieces of the same length.

Bas-Relief Decorations

Roll out the clay. Press a piece of lace or a coin into the clay and cut out the design: an image of the object will remain impressed in the clay.

 Work the clay on a sheet of glass, a smooth tile or on a sheet of plastic.

Using Craft Foam

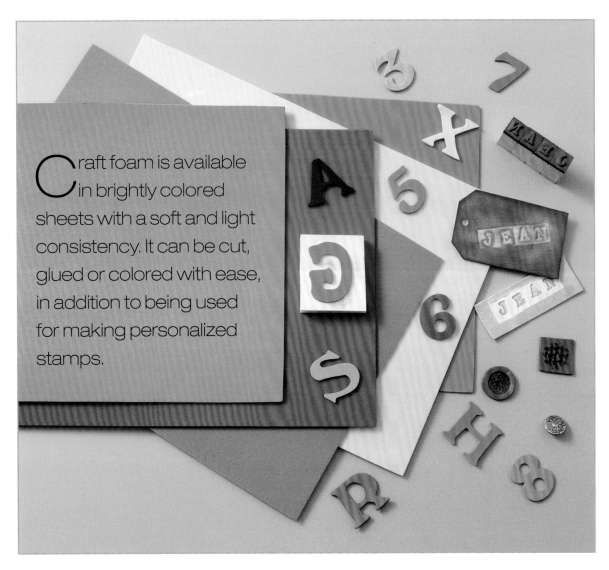

C raft foam is available in brightly colored sheets with a soft and light consistency. It can be cut, glued or colored with ease, in addition to being used for making personalized stamps.

Craft foam is widely available in stores: you can find it in A4 format sheets (as well as larger sheets) with thicknesses of 1/16 in. (1-2 mm) and up in a great variety of colors.

Suggestion

Make Personalized Stamps

To make your own stamps cut a design from craft foam. Glue the cutout onto a piece of foam board, coat with ink and stamp. If you want to use the stamp often, glue it onto a piece of Plexiglas: this way you can clean it with ease. Stamps made from craft foam are particularly good for use with acrylic paint.

1 - Cut

Draw a rectangle on a 1/16 in. (2 mm) thick sheet of white craft foam with a pencil. Cut out with scissors and trim two corners to form a label. Make a hole with a punch and hammer from a riveting kit.

2 - Heat

Compose writing with alphabet stamps and secure the stamps together with adhesive tape. Ink the stamps with a tea dye Distress ink pad. Heat the craft foam uniformly with an embossing gun. As soon as the foam begins to collapse, turn off the embossing gun.

3 - Stamp

Stamp immediately with force: an impression of the writing will remain on the craft foam. Allow the label to cool and the ink to dry.

4 - Ink

Tap a tea dye Distress ink pad over the entire surface of the label. Using a dark brown ink pad, ink the edges of the label. The final result is truly surprising: you have created a leather label with heat-impressed writing!

5 - Cut Out and Color

Craft foam can be shaped with decorative edge scissors and painted with acrylic paint. The example above shows a "cookie" frame made from a sheet of yellow craft foam. Scallop-edge scissors were used to cut out the edges. The acrylic paint used is red ochre. Points were made with a nail. The edges were stained with a dark brown ink pad.

You can also make other impressed designs using buttons or patterned stamps following steps 1 to 4.

Metal Foil

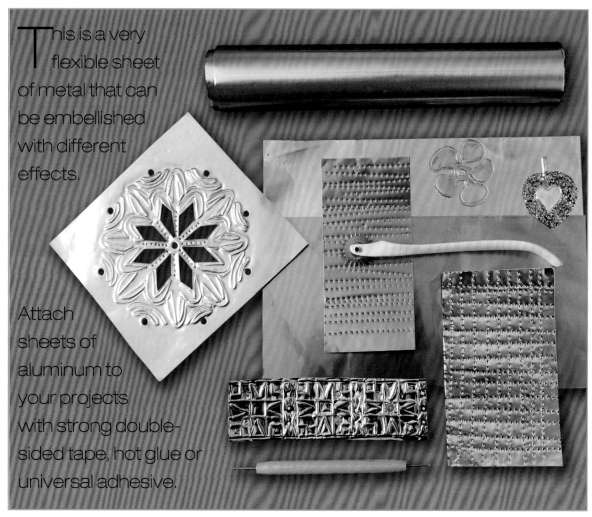

This is a very flexible sheet of metal that can be embellished with different effects.

Attach sheets of aluminum to your projects with strong double-sided tape, hot glue or universal adhesive.

Metal foil can be made of copper, brass or aluminum (the latter may be natural or colored). They are available in sheets or rolls and have a thickness of 1/10 of a millimeter.

Suggestion

Decorating with Embossed Elements

Color embossed motifs with a StazOn solvent-based ink pad, which adheres well to smooth, non-porous surfaces. The vignette (photo above) was coated with red ink and decorated with sequins glued on with fast-drying adhesive. The heart (photo on the right) was stained with red ink and coated with fast-drying adhesive; the sequins were drizzled on the adhesive.

Positioning the Foil

Place a sheet of foam rubber onto a working surface. Position the metal foil and the sheet of tracing paper with the motif on top. Secure together with adhesive tape.

Making a Hole

To make clean and precise holes, use the punch and hammer from a riveting kit. Alternatively, use a large nail: the edges will turn inwards and the cut will be less regular producing a unique effect.

Embossing the Motif

Trace the drawing with an embossing stylus, a pen that has run out of ink, a nail etc. Depending on the tool chosen and the amount of pressure applied, you will get different effects.

Incising a Motif

To cut out a motif, place the foil on a suitable mat and use a utility knife: you can make clean cuts along the motif outline eliminating excess foil or you can cut a cross in the center and fold the foil flaps onto the back of the sheet.

Making a Dotted Line

A dotted line can prove particularly decorative. To make it, you can use a pricking wheel. If you don't have this tool, attach a piece of masking tape to the foil and make a series of equally spaced holes with a large needle using the edge of the tape as a guide.

Cutting the Foil

To cut out the outline of the motif, use decoupage scissors or a utility knife. If you use a utility knife, make sure the blade is new, particularly if the foil is very thin, otherwise you risk ruining it.

The pricking wheel is a tool composed of rotating teethed wheel that is used by shoemakers to mark the location of stitches on leather used to make shoes.

Adhesive Tapes

Each project calls for its own pressure-activated adhesive, which may be repositionable or not, in the form of a tape or precut squares.

1
Clear Adhesive Tape

2
Kraft Gummed Paper Packaging Tape

3
Double-Sided Tape

4
Removable Tape

5
Masking Tape

6
Decorative Tape

7
Double-Sided Tape Dispenser

8
Decorative Tape

Give Preference to Adhesives with a Neutral pH for creations you wish to remain unaltered in time: albums, cards, scrapbook pages. The product should be labeled acid free.

If the packaging has no such writing, the adhesive is acidic.

Securing Small Decorations and Adhering Delicate Paper.

To attach transparent, parchment or extremely thin paper, or to secure small objects or decorations to your scrapbook pages and projects, adhesive tape is by far the most effective: liquid glue can overflow the edges or stain the paper, while spray adhesive is not recommended for very small decorations.

1 Clear Adhesive Tape

Used above all in drafting because it's invisible on tracing paper. Once applied, it can be written on with pens, pencils and permanent markers.

2 Kraft Gummed Paper Packaging Tape

It's composed of a Kraft paper backing coated with fast-drying adhesive which is activated when moistened with a sponge. Its strength makes it ideal for packaging, especially for reinforcing the corners of cardboard boxes.

3, 7 and 11 Double-Sided Tape

Indispensable for gluing delicate paper, photographs or small decorations, it is available in rolls but also as precut squares, which make it easier to handle, especially when assembling small objects.

4 Removable Tape

Ideal for testing out different compositions or for final assembly because it can be easily detached and repositioned without damaging the paper.

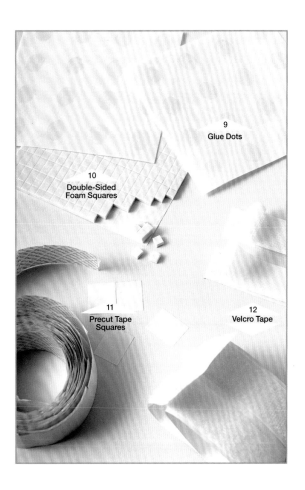

5 Masking Tape

Made using semi-crepe paper, this tape is ideal for masking off areas where you don't want the paint to go when painting different surfaces. You can also use it to temporarily attach paper and photographs, or to keep two sheets together while tracing.

6 and 8 Decorative Tape

Patterned or metallic, decorative tapes will give a special touch to your projects (presents, cards and so on) personalizing them in an original and creative way!

TRICK. *Store the permanent and repositionable adhesive materials in separate boxes, because they can be difficult to distinguish once removed from their original packaging.*

9 Glue Dots

Invisible glue dots (they appear as a sheet of paper with rows of "dots" of glue) are ideal for securing small decoration and gluing thin, transparent paper. They are available in different sizes.

10 Double-Sided Foam

A thick, double-sided adhesive, it is available as tape or in pre-cut squares of various sizes. It is used as a spacer between images and decorations, and their backing.

12 Velcro Tape

It is a self-adhesive, pull-apart, hook-and-loop tape composed of two components, one containing hooks and the other loops, which join when pressed together (to separate them, it is sufficient to tear one component from the other). Velcro can be used to construct fun greeting cards that can be opened and sealed as many times as you like!

Glues

The quality of your creations depends, in part, on how they are glued together: the adhesive must be suitable to the backing and the object or materials being glued; the bond must be solid and durable. To avoid unpleasant surprises, choose the most suitable type of adhesive for the foreseen assembly.

Suggestion

Repositionable Adhesive

This adhesive can be used on paper, cardboard and photographs, and is particularly useful for experimenting with compositions or page layouts because it allows the different elements to be moved before being attached definitively.

(A) Repositionable Spray Adhesive
(B) Permanent Spray Adhesive
(C) Glue Gun and Glue Sticks
(D) All-in-One Glue and Sealer
(E) Elmer's Glue
(F) Glitter glue
(G) Epoxy (resin+hardener)
(H) Neoprene-Based Adhesive
(I) Rubber Cement
(J) Glue Pen
(K) Universal Fast-Drying Adhesive
(L) Super Glue
(M) Glue stick

Gluing Small Surfaces

For gluing paper, cardboard and photographs, use a glue stick or a glue pen. To attach small components, place them onto the surface of the glue stick then transfer them to their final positions using tweezers, to avoid getting glue on your fingers or the backing.

Gluing Large Surfaces

For gluing large surfaces, apply a thin, even coat of spray adhesive. Elmer's glue ensures perfect, long-lasting assemblages, but may be inconvenient because of its water content, which requires a period of drying (on a flat surface, under a weight for flat assemblages and outside for three-dimensional assemblages).

Gluing Different Materials

To glue wood, leather, metal or cork objects to a backing, use a neoprene-based adhesive. Apply lines of adhesive to the back of the object and to the backing. Allow to dry then press the two elements together: the bond is instant and strong.

Assembling 3D Objects

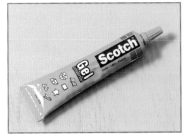

For such projects, choose a universal fast-drying adhesive. Apply the adhesive, assemble and press together for a few seconds. Clean the edges with a finger. If in spite of your efforts, a spot of dried glue should compromise the quality of your work, use a nail file to remove it.

Decoupage Projects

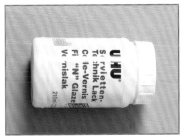

All-in-one glue and sealer is indispensable for gluing rice paper sheets or Decopatch paper: once dry, it forms a waterproof protective film on the surface. To better protect the surface of a decorated object, always apply an extra layer of all-in-one glue and sealer.

Gluing Other Objects

To glue irregularly shaped or heavy objects (pebbles, shells, beads etc.) you may choose to use hot glue gun (the glue stick is inserted into the gun, which melts it and expels it through the nozzle; as the glue cools it solidifies and joins the two components together), epoxy (it has two components, the resin and the hardener, which must be mixed before use) or super glue (just one drop and a few seconds are enough to securely glue together different materials; use it with caution, or you will find yourself with fingers glued to the backing or to each other!)

Decorative Gluing

Glue may also be visible and complementary to the decoration: glitter-glue tubes, which are used like a pen, can be used to attach small objects and create sparkling designs!

Gluing Tracing Paper

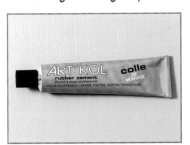

For an invisible bond that does not cause tracing paper to warp, use Rubber Cement, a fast-drying adhesive composed of natural rubber and a solvent (such as acetone, hexane, heptane or benzene).

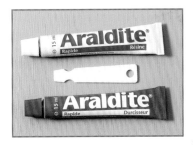

The Techniques

The Color Wheel

Make a color wheel to help you identify primary and secondary colors, warm tones, cold tones and intermediate tones. It will be useful in planning a project, choosing the most suitable colors and creating harmonious color combinations.

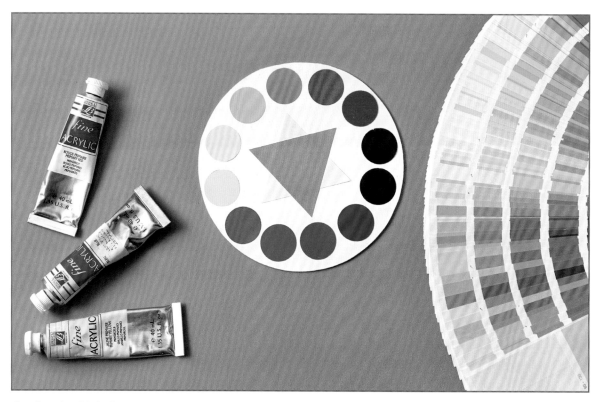

A color wheel is built around the three primary colors: cyan, magenta and yellow.

Suggestion

Primary Colors

Primary colors are cyan (a color similar to blue), magenta (similar to a bright pink) and yellow. From these three colors, it is possible to obtain all the other colors of the color wheel.

Secondary Colors

Mixing pairs of primary colors produces secondary colors: cyan + yellow = green; cyan + magenta = purple; magenta + yellow = red.

Tertiary Colors

Tertiary colors are obtained by mixing equal amounts of primary and secondary colors. The number of tertiary colors is practically infinite: just mix two adjacent colors to get a third color.

1 - Prepare the Wheel

Cut out a circle with a diameter of 6 1/4 in. (16 cm) from white card stock. Cut two equilateral triangles with 2 3/4 in. (7 cm) sides: one from a gray card stock and one from light gray card stock. Glue the triangles to the center of the circle, overlapping them to form a six-pointed star.

2 - Paint the Primary Colors

On white card stock, paint one yellow, one magenta and one cyan strips. Punch out a circle from each strip with a craft punch. Glue the circles next to the tips of the dark gray triangle.

3 - Paint the Secondary Colors

On white card stock, paint strips of color mixing equal amounts of yellow and cyan for the green, cyan and magenta for the purple, and magenta and yellow for the red. Punch out circles of each color and glue them next to the tips of the light gray triangle.

IDEA. You can make other color wheels using markers, acrylic paint, chalk etc. You will need color samples for your projects.

4 - Paint the Tertiary Colors

Mix, also in equal amounts, two adjacent colors and use them to paint strips: yellow + red, red + magenta, magenta + purple, purple + cyan, cyan + green, green + yellow. Punch out circles of each color and glue them between the other circles.

5 - Identify the Warm and Cold Colors

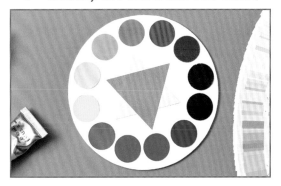

The wheel is divided into two equal halves: warm colors on one side (yellow, orange and red) and cold colors on the other (purple, blue and green).

Black and White

Black and white are not part of the color wheel: they are neutral colors that serve to modify the brightness of the other colors (in the photo below, magenta is being mixed with white and black to form two color scales). Combining white and black produces gray: by varying the proportions of these colors, very light and very dark grays can be obtained.

Choosing Colors

Choosing the best color scheme for a scrapbooking page, card or frame is not easy: from where should you start? You can start from the main colors of the photo or paper for example. Create a color scheme most pleasing to you with the help of a color wheel.

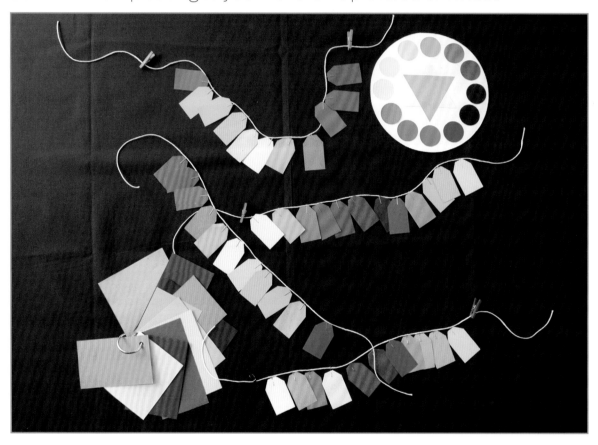

Suggestion

Color "Temperature"

Warm Colors. Warm colors include red, orange and yellow. Warm colors are brighter to the eye and associated with the sun and its heat.

Cold Colors. Cold colors include green, blue and purple. These colors are associated with the sea and the sky.

Analogous Combinations

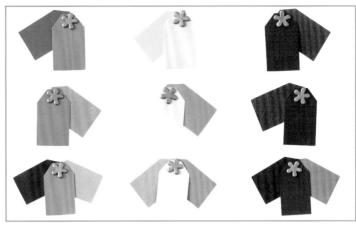

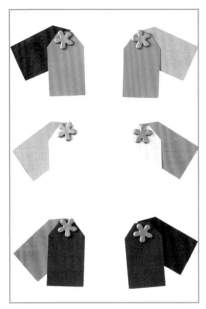

These color combinations are made by pairing a primary color with one or more secondary or tertiary colors formed by mixing the chosen primary color with another color (primary or secondary) from the color wheel. For example, yellow and orange.

Complementary Combinations

These color combinations are made by pairing a primary color with one or more complementary secondary colors, or with one secondary color and one complementary secondary color.

Triadic Combinations

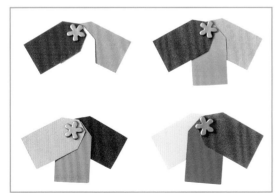

You can also pair three colors that form an equilateral triangle on the color wheel.

It is best to choose one dominant color and use the others for the details and decorations.

Color Gradations

You can also choose to use different gradations of just one color.

Hand-made Paper

Create original sheets of paper starting from regular or used paper. To make color paper you will need to add ink. To decorate them, on the other hand, embed with leaves or flowers, embroidery thread, glitter etc. To start, we suggest making small sheets of paper.

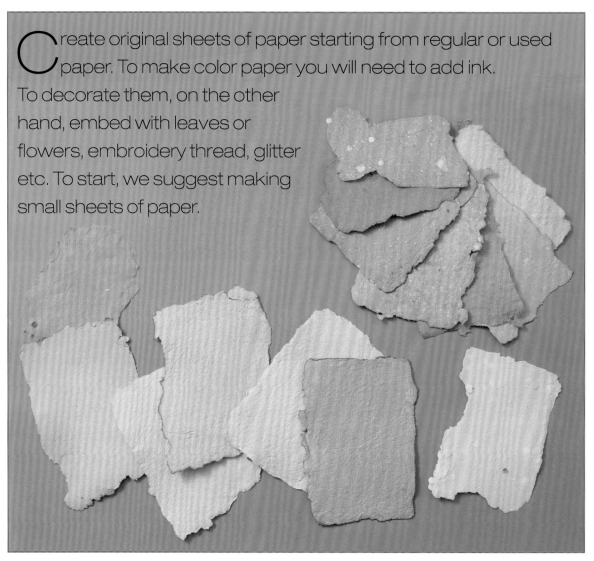

The lightest-color samples were made using printing paper and the beige, using Kraft paper. To make color paper just add a little bit of ink to light-colored pulp.

1 - Prepare the Pulp

Take used paper (Kraft paper, printing paper, scraps of one tone color paper and so on) and rip it into small pieces. Place the pieces of paper into a basin full of warm water. Allow to soak for two hours. Using a blender, blend the softened pieces of paper adding one tablespoon of cornstarch as a thickener.

2 - Prepare the Sieve

Place several layers of moist newspaper sheets into a container, making sure there are no wrinkles. Put a damp cloth on top. Using a stapler attach a piece of mosquito netting to a wood frame to form a sieve.

3 - Shape the Sheet

Dip the sieve into the container with the slurry allowing an evenly distributed layer of pulp to deposit on top. Allow excess water to drip for a few moments without shaking.

4 - Deposit the Sheet

Flip the sieve onto the pile of newspaper sheets and the damp cloth (this is the most delicate step: if the sheet of paper pulp should "break," you must start over). Place a second moist cloth on top. If you want, you can prepare other sheets repeating steps 1-3 and piling them on top of the first (place a moist cloth between each sheet).

5 - Press

Put dry newspapers on the bottom of a flat-bottomed container. Place the sheet of paper sandwiched between pieces of cloth on top. Position a board (for example, a cutting board) on top and step on it to eliminate excess water.

6 - Allow to Dry

Take off the board and the newspapers, leaving just the sheet sandwiched between two pieces of cloth. Allow to dry completely. Gently detach the pieces of cloth to avoid tearing the paper.

Making Paper with Embedded Material

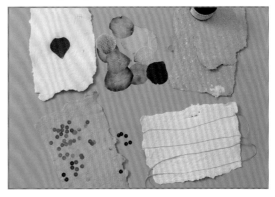

Embedding plant material, glitter, string, spangles, powdered spices or colored ink can render your handmade paper unique and original! Vary the effect achieved by adding the material directly into the pulp or in step 4.

Paper Mache

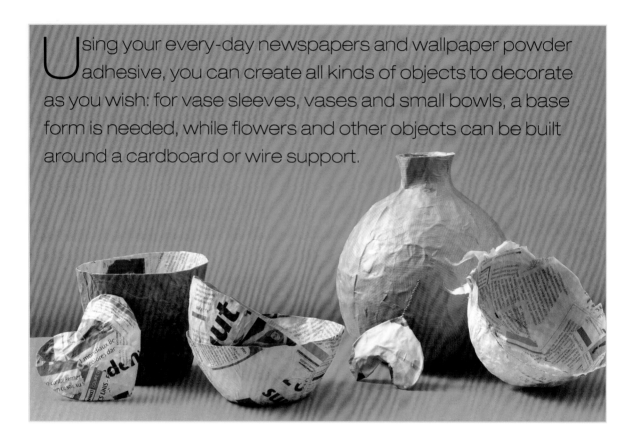

Using your every-day newspapers and wallpaper powder adhesive, you can create all kinds of objects to decorate as you wish: for vase sleeves, vases and small bowls, a base form is needed, while flowers and other objects can be built around a cardboard or wire support.

Suggestion

Paper Mache Different Objects

You can paper mache many different objects, including balls and inflated balloons, but also bottles. In the latter case, since it is impossible to remove the cast, you will have to incise it with a utility knife, break into halves and extract the base form. To reconstruct the paper mache object, just join the halves together with other strips of glue-soaked paper soaked.

CAST OF AN OBJECT

Prepare the Paper

Dilute the wallpaper powder adhesive as indicated on the packaging. Cover the base form with plastic wrap. Rip a newspaper into small pieces and dip them into the wallpaper paste. Lay the strips of paper onto the base form overlapping them slightly.

Cover the Base Form

Cover with several layers of paper. The bigger the base form, the more layers of paper you will have to lay for the cast to be sufficiently rigid. Allow to dry for at least 24 hours before extracting.

Remove the Cast

Extract the base form and the clear plastic wrap. Trim the edge of the cast with scissors. Apply a layer of white acrylic paint or gesso to the cast. Allow to dry. It can be painted or covered with tissue paper glued with Elmer's glue or with two-in-one glue and sealer.

CREATING VOLUME

Prepare the Support Structure

Cut out the desired shape from a piece of cardboard or make a support structure from metal wire. A little at a time, coat the support with small pieces of paper dipped in the dilute glue.

Add Volume

To give a three-dimensional effect, rip small pieces of newspaper, bunch them up and position in the spots where you want more volume. Cover with pieces of paper soaked in glue. Allow to dry. Apply a layer of white acrylic paint or gesso. Decorate as you wish.

Suggestion

You can make the cast using drawing paper of medium grammage. Dip the pieces of paper in glue allowing them to soak for a bit longer, so that all the fibers have time to soften. Proceed as described. Leave the resulting cast as is or paint it.

Covering Card Stock

To make an album, a frame or a box, you must cover the card stock with paper: cut the paper to the right size and glue it on with a thin and even coat of Elmer's glue. Once learned, you can use this technique to cover all of your creations, both flat and three-dimensional, with little effort.

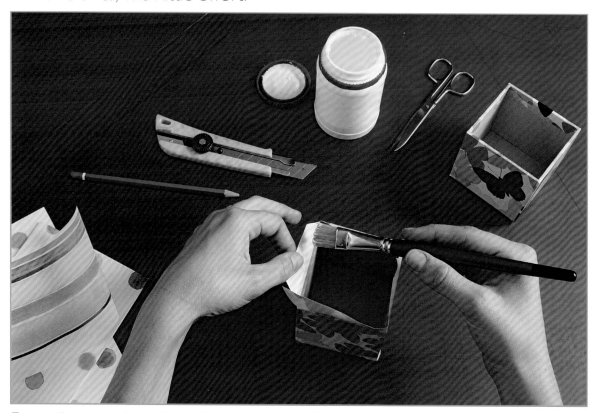

To cover the corners of a cardboard object properly, a specific cut must be made.

Drying

After gluing the sheet of paper onto the card stock, you must allow it to dry with a weight on top, especially if the card stock is not very thick, or it may warp irreparably.

Gluing Fabric

To cover card stock with fabric, spread the glue on the card stock, not the fabric. Give preference to fabrics with a fine weave (coarse weaves will produce ill-defined creases) made of cotton (synthetic fabrics don't bind easily and let the glue to pass through) fabrics.

COVERING CARD STOCK

Glue the Paper

Trace the card stock to be covered onto the back of a sheet of paper, adding a margin of about 3/4 in. (2 cm) all around. Cut the paper with a utility knife. Brush Elmer's glue onto the card stock and adhere the paper. Smooth with a cloth.

Cut the Corners

Cut away a triangle of paper from each corner (leave a margin equal to the thickness of the card stock by the tips of the corners). Brush glue onto the flaps an fold them over the edges with the help of a bone folder.

Cover the Back

Cut a rectangle of paper with dimensions of about 1/2 in. (1 cm) smaller than the card stock. Center and glue it to the back of the card stock. Smooth well and allow to dry under a weight.

COVERING A BOX

Glue the Paper

Cut a strip of paper with a length equal to the perimeter of the box plus about 1/2 in. (1 cm, the flap) and a width equal to the height of the box plus about 1 1/4 in. (3 cm). Glue the paper onto the box with Elmer's glue starting from the flap. Smooth each side as you work. Trim the paper flush with the card stock.

Glue the Upper Flaps

Using scissors, cut out triangles in correspondence with the corners (leave a margin of paper equal to the thickness of the card stock). Brush glue onto the four paper flaps and fold them over the edges of the box with a bone folder.

Glue the Lower Flaps

Cut triangles in correspondence with the corners (in this case, don't leave any margin). Brush glue onto the four flaps and fold over. Afterwards, cover the bottom and the inside of the box making sure to measure the height and width of each face accurately.

Gluing Paper Napkins

Among the incredibly vast range of traditional paper napkins, you are sure to find something suitable for covering a scrapbook page or a notebook cover; you can also cut out different motifs for decorating a frame or a lampshade and so on. All you need for an excellent result is a pair of decoupage scissors, a brush and a tub of decoupage glue for napkins!

Napkins can be cut or torn, depending on the design they contain, the surface to be covered and the effect desired.

Suggestion

Covering Large Surfaces

If you want to completely cover a greeting card or a scrapbook page with paper towels, there is a risk that the backing will warp. To circumvent this problem, there are several possible solutions: you can use a more rigid backing (cardboard or foam board); you can use a backing with higher grammage (heavier card stock); or you can allow the glue to dry slightly, lay a piece of parchment paper on top and allow the paper to dry completely under a weight.

1 - Prepare the Napkins

Napkins are composed of several layers of paper: separate the first layer (the one with the pattern) from those below it (white) by inserting a nail under one corner or crumpling the center of the napkin to part the layers, and remove it.

2 - Gluing the Paper

Cut out the desired motif with sharp, short-blade scissors. Apply decoupage glue for napkins to the backing. Lay the paper over the backing starting from one end by gently smoothing it down with a brush, making sure not to leave any wrinkles or air bubbles.

3 - Protecting Your Work

Allow to dry and apply another coat of glue to the surface.

Gluing Large Motifs

Cut out the chosen motif with decoupage scissors. Gently glue it to the backing as described in steps 2 and 3.

Patchwork Gluing

To create interesting visual effects, mix regular and irregular, cut and torn pieces of napkins. Stagger and overlap them randomly for a unique effect. Glue on as described in steps 2 and 3.

Gluing Very Small Motifs

For very small components, cut leaving a margin around the image. Glue on as described in steps 2 and 3 onto a white sheet. Allow to dry. Cut out with decoupage scissors. Glue onto the chosen backing with decoupage glue for napkins without worrying about it tearing.

Sewing Paper by Hand

With just a few stitches you can "enrich" a scrapbook page, decorate a card, sew together several sheets of paper or frame a photograph. Whatever the stitch or the thread chosen, paper cannot be sewn like fabric: you must prepare the design, transfer it onto paper and make holes for the thread to pass through.

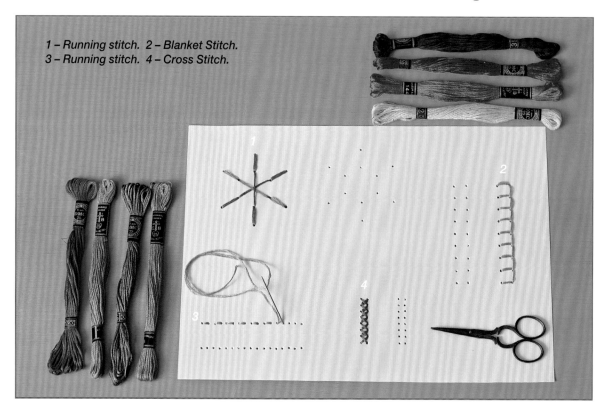

1 – Running stitch. 2 – Blanket Stitch.
3 – Running stitch. 4 – Cross Stitch.

Suggestion

The Needles

The needles are distinguished by their diameter, their tips (rounded or sharp) and their eyes (the loop through which the thread is passed). For sewing paper, the shape of the tip is unimportant because the needle is inserted into premade holes. Choose a needle with an appropriate size eye for the thread being used: a standard thin needle is best for sewing thread; for cotton, wool, twine or raffia, choose a needle with an eye big enough for the thread to pass without forcing.

Prepare the Paper:
Simple Stitching

To sew a running or a backstitch, draw a line on the paper with a pencil. Mark reference points along the line with the help of a ruler: decide on an even distance between the marks based on how long you want the stitch to be (1/8 in. /3 mm, 1/4 in. /5 mm, etc.)

Prepare the Paper:
Complex Stitching

To do a cross stitch or a blanket stitch, attach a strip of graph paper to the paper with removable tape. Mark the perforation points with a red pen. If you have to embroider a motif (flower, leaf etc.), trace the diagram of the design onto the paper.

Pierce and Sew:
Pierce the Paper

Using a sharp needle or a piercing tool, perforate the paper following the marks, or the points of the diagram or the graph paper. Before doing this, line the working surface with a foam rubber mat or a piece of foam board.

Pierce and Sew:
Start Sewing

Do not knot the end of the thread; a knot will result in a bump once the paper is glued to the backing. Use a piece of adhesive tape to secure the thread end to the back of the paper.

Pierce and Sew:
Change Threads and Secure the End

If your thread is too short for the entire length of the stitching, secure the end to the back with a piece of adhesive tape. Take another length of thread, secure it to the back with pieces of tape and continue stitching. When the stitching is complete, secure the end of the string to the back of the paper with another piece of adhesive tape. Cut away excess thread. Smooth the tape well with your nail. You can strengthen the stitching by positioning a strip of adhesive tape on the back of the paper over the entire length of the stitching.

 For piercing the paper, choose the tool (needle or piercing tool) based on the thickness of the thread that you will use for sewing or embroidering.

Decorative Stitches

Framing stitches such as the stem stitch or the chain stitch, lone stitches such as the star stitch or the French knot, or hemming stitches such as the blanket stitch: embroidery can add elegance to a scrapbook page or a card. Use several stitches, overlapping the threads and varying the colors: in this way, your results will be new, refined and surprising every time!

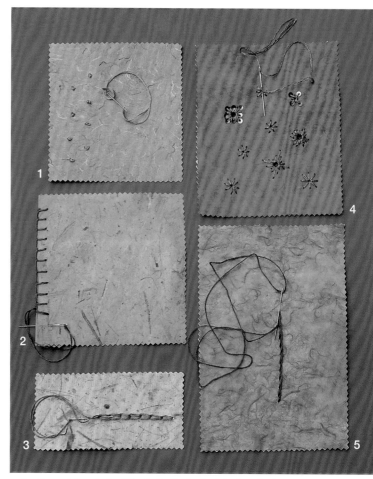

1 - French knot. 2 - Blanket stitch. 3 - Chain stitch.
4 - Star stitch. 5 - Stem stitch.

Suggestion

Embroider with Mouliné Cotton
This embroidery floss has the advantage of being composed of six different strands that can be conveniently separated: varying the number of strands used will give you very different results.

The French Knot

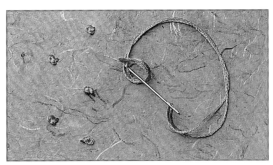

French knots can be aligned at even intervals to form a design, or positioned randomly. Pull the needle up through the fabric, twist the thread two or three times around the needle, tighten and pass the needle down through the paper close to where you pulled it up.

The Star Stitch

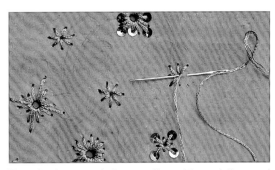

To make the star stitch, you will need to work it around a central opening. The dimensions of the central hole (made with a needle or a punch), the length and order of the stitches can be varied as desired. To make your stars sparkle, string sequins onto the thread!

The Blanket Stitch

The blanket stitch involves looping the thread around straight or curved edges. You can use spaced out stitches to bind small notebooks and closely spaced stitches for decorative borders.

The Stem Stitch

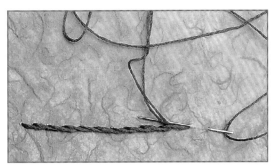

The stem stitch not only allows to bind many layers of paper or fabric, but can follow the most sinuous of curves perfectly. For an impressive result, overlay several lines of stitches.

The Chain Stitch

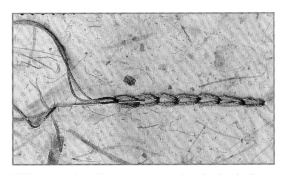

With the chain stitch, you can make simple designs: hearts, initials, flowers etc. Embroider a series of loops of the same lengths and finish by securing the last with a small running stitch.

Suggestion

When embroidering thin paper, make sure not to pull the thread too hard: place your finger under the paper to feel the tension being created. To work with wool or thicker thread, you will need a tapestry needle, which has a rounded tip. To avoid tearing the paper, pierce it with a sharp needle before embroidering.

Attaching Ribbons

There is a wide variety of ribbons (organza, satin, taffeta and cotton twill) of various colors and patterns on sale. In addition to making bows and knots, you can glue or sew them to add a decorative accent to scrapbook pages, cards etc. Choose the most suitable technique for your project: this is the only way to get a good result and an impeccable finish.

Suggestion

Secure a Ribbon with Paper Fasteners

Pierce the ribbon and the paper with a punch or a large needle. Insert a paper fastener. For taffeta ribbons, make sure to use a very sharp and smooth tool when piercing, to avoid pulling on the threads of the ribbon's fabric. To add rigidity to the ribbon, you can attach a strip of white paper slightly narrower than the ribbon to its back before piercing.

ATTACHMENT
Position the Ribbon

Place a ruler on the surface to decorate and secure it with pieces of removable tape. Position the ribbon flush with the edge of the ruler.

ATTACHMENT
Glue the Ribbon

Attach narrow ribbons with a glue stick. For wider ribbons (over 1/2 in.,1 cm), you can use double-sided tape.

ATTACHMENT
Sew the Ribbon

To sew a ribbon to paper, with a sewing machine or by hand, secure it with removable tape, which you will eliminate after sewing. Avoid using glue or double-sided tape, which may leave traces of glue on the needle.

FINISHING
Fold Over the Ends

If the ribbon has a tendency to fray, fold each end over the edges of the paper and secure with pieces of tape.

FINISHING
Incise the Paper

You can obtain a very clean finish by incising the paper about 1/2 in. (1 cm) from the edge (the length of the incision should correspond to the width of the ribbon). Insert the ends of the ribbon into the incisions and secure to the back of the paper with adhesive tape.

FINISHING
Cut the Ends

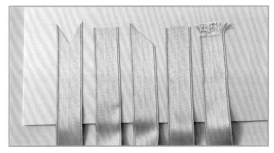

If you want, you can notch the ends of the ribbon, cut them straight, obliquely or with decorative-edge scissors (but only wide ribbons). The ends can also be frayed for about 1/2 in. (1 cm) of their length.

 The moisture contained in a glue stick can smooth out a very wrinkled ribbon. If you prefer to attach it with adhesive tape, on the other hand, it is best to iron it first.

Attaching Beads, Spangles & Co.

Sequins, glitter, gems, beads and mirrors are decorations that can add an extra touch to your creations: some can be glued, others sewn or simply pinned to their backing.

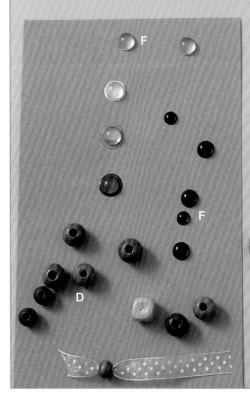

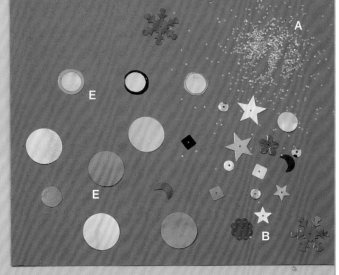

A - Glitter. B - Sequins. C - Seed Beads. D - Wood Beads. E - Mirrors. F - Gems.

Suggestion

Make Imitation Beads
Deposit small drops of dimensional acrylic paint onto the backing and allow it to dry thoroughly.

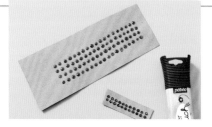

Make Do-It-Yourself Beads
Create your own beads using synthetic modeling clay and bake them in a home oven.

Glitter

Glitter can be applied to paper with glue. Using a pencil, trace an image onto a sheet of paper. Spread glue over the interior of the design. Position a sheet of scrap paper underneath the paper. Pour the glitter onto the drawing and make sure it adheres evenly. Gently shake off excess glitter onto the paper below and reuse for another project.

Wood Beads

Wood beards can be glued or strung on metal wire, fabric ribbon or embroidery thread.

Mirrors

Small decorative mirrors can be attached to a surface using fast-drying adhesive. To attach and embellish the mirrors at the same time, apply a little bit of dimensional acrylic paint onto the surface and place the mirror in the center: the paint will be pushed outwards creating a frame around the mirror. To make do-it-yourself mirrors, use foil for embossing and perforate it with the perforating tool and hammer from a riveting kit.

Sequins

Sequins can be glued onto paper with fast-drying adhesive or sewn on. To attach them to foam board or another backing surface of the same consistency (such as Styrofoam), you can use short pins.

Seed Beads

Seed beads can be glued with fast-drying adhesive, sewn or strung onto thin metal wire or embroidery thread, or even secured to foam board with short pins. To make gluing a row of seed beads easier, string them first onto a piece of metal wire. Apply a string of glue to the backing, adhere the beads and pull out the wire.

Gems

Gems can be attached to a surface with a fast-drying adhesive. If the gem is not very heavy and has to be attached to a rigid surface, such as cardboard, you can attach it with a piece of double-sided tape. Alternatively, use a little bit of dimensional acrylic paint, as with the mirrors.

Decorating with Sand

Colored sand can be used to create textured motifs on scrapbook pages, cards, frames and boxes. To glue the sand to the chosen surface, all you need is some Elmer's glue or double-sided tape.

Suggestion

Seed Beads

You can use colored or clear seed beads to make textured motifs. For the heart to the side do the following: color the inside of the heart with a blue marker, spread some fast-drying adhesive on top, turn over the sheet and place it on top of a plate full of blue seed beads. The current bunch is covered with clear seed beads.

DECORATING WITH MOTIFS
Drawn Motifs

Draw a motif on a square of white card stock freehand or trace using tracing paper. Position the square on a piece of scrap paper. Using a brush, apply a uniform layer of Elmer's glue inside the traced image. Sprinkle the sheet of paper with colored sand. Shake off the excess.

Punched Out Motifs

Perforate a double-sided adhesive sheet with a craft punch. Place a square of card stock onto a sheet of scrap paper. Stick the punched-out image onto the card stock. Sprinkle with colored sand. Shake off the excess.

Adding Texture to an Image

Using decoupage glue attach an image cut out from a napkin onto a piece of paper. Allow to dry. Place onto a sheet of scrap paper. Using a brush, apply Elmer's glue to the portions of the image where you want some texture. Sprinkle with colored sand. Allow to dry. Repeat if there are other parts of the image that you wish to coat with differently colored sand. Shake off excess sand.

GEOMETRIC DECORATIONS
Creating Colored Stripes

Stick strips of double-sided tape (to decorate with sand of the same color) onto paper. Place the paper onto a sheet of scrap paper. Sprinkle with colored sand. Stick on other strips of double-sided tape (to decorate with sand of a different color) and repeat the process. Shake the paper to remove excess sand.

Creating Patterns

Stick strips of double-sided tape onto an object. Remove the protective backing from strips to decorate with the same color. Sprinkle the object with sand. Shake off the excess. Remove the protective film from strips to decorate with a different color, sprinkle with sand and so on.

After having finished working, spray on a coat of clear matte spray paint to secure the sand to the surface further.

Using Distress Ink Pads

D istress inks, in combination with water, allow to obtain interesting textures on simple sheets of white paper. Crumple, fold, ink (mixing colors together if desired), spray with water, emboss, or stamp with stamps: a different effect every time!

1 – Solid faux finish. 2 – Crumpled finish. 3 – Crumpled and re-inked finish. 4 – Stamped finish. 5 – Folded and re-inked finish.

Solid Faux Finish

Drag a Distress Ink pad over the paper. Using a flat brush loaded with water spread the ink evenly in line with the desired effect.

Crumpled Finish

Prepare a sheet with a solid faux finish and allow to dry. Crumple the sheet of paper into a ball. Open it back up and smooth it out well with the palm of your hand.

Crumpled and Re-Inked Finish

Using a Distress Ink pad "smear" the most prominent wrinkles of a crumpled sheet with ink.

Folded and Re-Inked Finish

Prepare a sheet with a solid faux finish and allow to dry. Fold and "stain" the creases with a Distress Ink pad.

Embossed Finish

Stamp a pattern with a clear ink pad on a white piece of paper. Sprinkle with clear or white embossing powder. Bind with an embossing gun. Drag a Distress Ink pad over the paper. Spread water over the surface with a flat brush: the embossed designs will suddenly become visible!

Ink-Transfer Finish

Dab Distress Ink pads of different colors on a sheet of acetate. Flip the acetate over onto a sheet of white paper. Press down and smooth the acetate to transfer the ink onto the paper.

Stamped Finish

Prepare a sheet with a solid faux finish. Stamp the still moist sheet with a stamp coated with Distress Ink or any other ink pad impregnated with a slow-drying ink.

At the end of every project, iron the paper to flatten any irregularities and to set the color.

Gilding

Use gilding to embellish all of your projects. There are numerous products on sale: from acrylic paint to wax, from metallic paper to gold leaf and so on. Depending on the material used, you will have to cut, glue, paint with a brush or use a stencil to create the designs of your choice.

A - Marker. B - Glitter glue.
C - Gold metallic paper. D - Glitter. E - Gold leaf.

Suggestion

Choose the Right Hue

There are many different shades of gold, from light gold to dark, from silvery gold to coppery gold: light gold, dark gold, yellow gold, antique gold etc. Choose the tone that fits your project best: the darker, more coppery tones are "warmer."

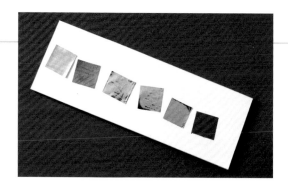

Gold Acrylic Paint, Markers and Spray Paint

Draw or copy and trace the design onto a backing. To color the design with acrylic paint or a marker, start with the outline and then fill in the interior. If you want to use gold spray paint, you will need to make a stencil from a sheet of acetate.

Gilding Wax

Gold paste is used mainly with stencils: secure the stencil to the work surface with adhesive tape and rub the wax across it with a finger. Remove the stencil and allow to dry. For geometric designs, mark the outline with strips of masking tape.

Gold Glitter and Powder

Coat the interior of the design with glue. Sprinkle the glitter or powder on top. Shake excess off onto a piece of paper. Curve the paper to form a funnel and pour the extra glitter or powder into a container. Allow to dry.

Gold Metallic Paper

Draw or copy and trace the motif onto the back of the gold paper. Cut out with scissors. Smear glue onto the back of the cutout with a glue stick and glue it. Place a piece of scrap paper over the motif and smooth well with your fingers.

Gold Leaf

Apply gilding size to the surface to be gilded. Allow to dry: the surface should be slightly sticky to the touch. Apply the gold leaf over the size, avoiding touching it with your hands. Place a piece of scrap paper onto the motif and smooth with your fingers. Allow to dry then eliminate excess leaf with a dry flexible brush. Apply a coat of sealer (glossy or matte) to protect the surface.

Gold Dimensional Paint and Glitter Glue

To draw lines, letters or very small motifs, use dimensional paint or glitter glue: their narrow nozzles, will enable you to make extremely precise drawings.

Dry Embossing

This is a technique that allows to create a motif in relief on paper or metal foil.

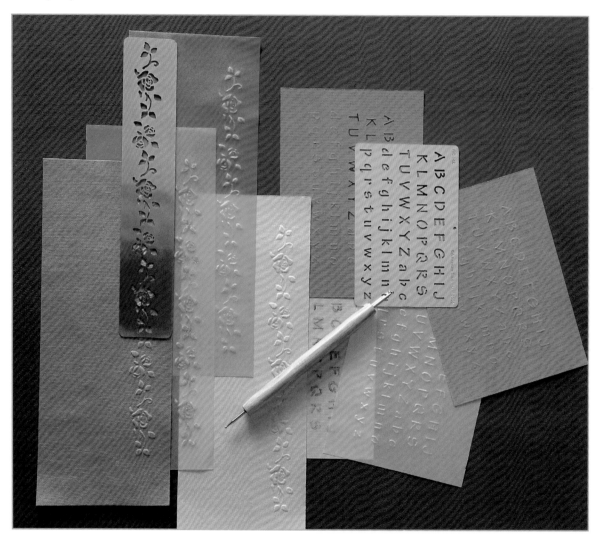

Dry embossing can be done on regular paper, translucent paper, veil paper or card stock.

The Light Box
In addition to embossing, a light box can be used for copying drawings or choosing your projection slides. Make one yourself by positioning a light under a glass surface.

Coloring the Motifs
You can color the motifs in relief using colored chalk and cotton balls, or using eye shadow and a cotton swab.

1 - Place All You Need Onto the Light Box

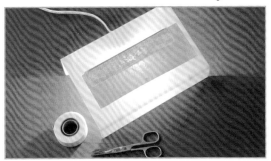

Place a sheet of paper onto the light box. Position the embossing stencil on top. Secure everything with a strip of removable tape.

2 - Embossing a Motif

The embossing stylus has a tip with a different diameter at each end: choose the tip that suits the size of the chosen motif best. Perform circular motions with the tip of the stylus inside the stencil opening, applying light pressure.

3 - Embossing Text

When embossing letters, be sure to position the template with the back facing up!

4 - Coloring Motifs with Chalk

Place the embossed paper onto a working surface with the elevated motif facing up. Position the template on top, aligning the design. Secure both with a strip of removable tape. Color every motif with chalk using cotton balls.

5 - Coloring Letters with Markers

Place the embossed paper onto a working surface with the elevated writing facing up. Position the template on top, aligning the letters. Secure both with a strip of removable tape. Trace each letter with a marker (choose a marker with the most suitable tip for the stencil openings). Allow to dry.

When embossing on a thick paper or metal foil, use an embossing kit that includes a base, templates and double-ended stylus.

Hot Embossing

This is a decorative technique for making motifs in relief. It uses a powder that is sprinkled over partially dry ink and heated with an embossing gun (hot air gun): as it melts, the powder fuses with the paper creating a relief.

Suggestion

Choosing Between Clear or Colored Embossing Powders

If your motif is colored, use clear powder (translucent opaline; glossy clear; translucent gold pearl; translucent pearl; clear glossy sparkle; translucent silver pearl; clear sparkle). Colored powder will mask the color of the ink used for stamping. If you used a clear ink pad, opt for opaque powders (metallic, glittery, or with a velvet finish).

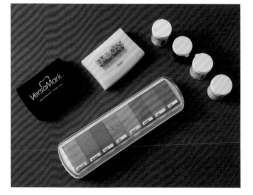

1 - Stamp

Place a used piece of paper onto the working surface. Dab the stamp on the ink pad. Stamp the design on the chosen paper surface. Generally, all ink pads are suitable for this technique, even though ink pads made for embossing have slow-drying inks.

2 - Pour the Powder

Sprinkle the stamped design with an abundant amount of embossing powder. Tap the paper on the underlying sheet of used paper to remove excess powder. Pour the excess powder into a container.

3 - Clean the Edges

Using a fine-tipped brush, remove any remaining bits of embossing powder from around the design. Gently blow on the paper.

4 - Fuse the Powder

Turn on the embossing gun and heat the powder until it starts to melt, making sure not to hold the gun too close to the paper, or you risk burning it! Make tight circular motions with the gun. As soon as the powder has melted, turn off the gun and allow the powder to cool.

Embossing Freehand with a Marker

To emboss a pre-existing design or text, pass over the motifs or the letters with an embossing marker (available clear or in different colors) and proceed from step 2.

Embossing with Texture Stamps

You can create an embossed pattern using texture stamps as well: gently dab the ink pad on the elevated surface of the stamp and proceed from step 2.

Do-It-Yourself Stamps

With a small amount of materials (twine, corrugated paper, craft foam and carving rubber) and a few tools (decoupage scissors, precision knife and carving tools) you can make original stamps for decorating your projects.

Stamping with Do-It-Yourself Stamps

All stamps made from craft foam or carving rubber can be used with acrylic paint or ink pads, which means they can also be used for hot embossing.

Twine and corrugated paper stamps can only be used with acrylic paint. In every case, make sure to test the stamps on scrap paper to assess the result.

Twine

Twine allows you to obtain simple decorations such as spirals, hearts or waves. Draw a motif on a piece of foam board with a pencil. Apply a line of fast-drying adhesive along the pencil mark and glue on the twine. Turn over the stamp and press it against the working surface for a few seconds to allow the twine to adhere better. Coat with acrylic paint using a sponge brush. These stamps don't last very long.

Corrugated Paper

Using corrugated paper, you can create original patterns for your scrapbook pages. Cut the corrugated paper into a simple shape, preferably geometric, then glue it onto a piece of foam board of the same size. Coat in acrylic paint. After repeated stamping, the ribbing will "soften": if you need to make a long border, prepare many similar stamps.

Suggestion

Keep cotton swabs and blotting paper within reach at all times. Cotton swabs will serve to clean stamp edges of excess ink before stamping, while blotting paper will serve to remove any remaining ink from stamps before cleaning.

Use carving rubber to make a stamp with your initials: you can use it to personalize all of your projects!

Carving Rubber

It is suitable for creating very small designs, letters, textures for backgrounds etc. Linoleum, a flexible material that is suitable to carving, is also often used for carving stamps. Before all else, the design must be drawn freehand on the piece of rubber or transferred using tracing paper. Next, it must be carved using a carving gouge. A gauge is a carving tool with a blade that is available in different shapes, even "U" and "V"-shaped. If the rubber is thick enough, you will not need to attach it to a backing otherwise, before stamping, you will need to glue it to a piece of wood or other material. These stamps can be easily inked with ink pads. Wash them with soapy water and dry them well: they will last a long time.

Craft Foam

Craft foam allows to create precise and relatively complex motifs, such as flowers, foliage and letters. Draw a design onto a sheet of craft foam. Cut it out using sharp decoupage scissors or a precision knife, and glue it to a piece of foam board. Ink with ink pads or coat in acrylic paint. These stamps, if cleaned with a moist sponge, can be reused many times.

For the English edition:

WHITE STAR PUBLISHERS

WS White Star Publishers® is a registered trademark
belonging to De Agostini Libri S.p.A.

Translation and Editing: TperTradurre S.R.L.

© 2015 De Agostini Libri S.p.A.
Via G. da Verrazano, 15
28100 Novara, Italy
www.whitestar.it - www.deagostini.it

ISBN 978-88-544-0955-2
1 2 3 4 5 6   19 18 17 16 15

Printed in China